Learn C

Practical Guide

A. De Quattro

Copyright © 2024

Practical Guide

1.Introduction

What is the C Language?

The C programming language is one of the oldest and most influential languages still in use in computer programming today. Developed in the 1970s, C has had a profound and lasting impact on many modern languages such as C++, Java, Python, and even JavaScript. It is considered a low-level or "middle-level" language, as it provides both direct access to hardware (typical of assembly languages) and high-level abstractions that simplify the development of complex software.

C is an imperative language, meaning that programs written in C are executed as a sequence of instructions that modify the system's state. This programming model, combined with its close relationship to computer hardware architecture, makes it ideal for developing operating systems, hardware drivers, programming languages, and other applications where efficiency and direct control of system resources are crucial.

One of the most appreciated aspects of the C language is its simplicity and portability. While powerful and complex, its syntax is relatively small and consistent, allowing programmers to easily understand how the code works. Additionally, since C is a standardized language (under the ISO C standard), programs written in C can be run on a wide range of platforms with minimal changes.

Moreover, C has a static type system, which allows the compiler to check the consistency of the code before it is executed, reducing the risk of runtime errors. C is also known for its direct use of pointers, a mechanism that enables precise and efficient manipulation of memory addresses and hardware resources, though this can also increase code complexity and the risk of bugs.

In summary, the C language is a fundamental

tool in the programming world due to its speed, power, and control, making it a popular choice for developing critical software in industrial and academic settings.

History of the C Language

The history of the C language is closely tied to the development of early modern operating systems and computer science itself. C was created by Dennis Ritchie at Bell Labs in 1972, and its development was intertwined with UNIX, an operating system that has had an extraordinary influence on the entire landscape of modern operating systems.

The 1960s: BCPL and B

Before the C language was born, there were several programming languages. One of the most relevant to C's history was BCPL (Basic Combined Programming Language), developed by Martin Richards in 1966. BCPL was designed to be simple and to facilitate writing compilers and operating systems, inspiring another language, B, created by Ken Thompson in 1969, also at Bell Labs.

The B language was the direct predecessor of C. Thompson used it to write one of the early versions of the UNIX operating system on a PDP-7 computer, but it soon became clear that B had limitations, particularly in terms of efficiency and control over hardware resources. It was in response to these limitations that Dennis Ritchie began developing the C language, evolving the ideas of B and adding new features.

The 1970s: The Birth of C

In 1972, the C language came to life with its first complete implementation, developed by Ritchie. C was designed to be used with the UNIX system, and both developed and grew together. This connection between UNIX and the C language was crucial for the latter's popularity and spread: the fact that UNIX was written in C made it highly portable, as it was only necessary to port the C compiler to new hardware to run UNIX on it.

The portability of C and UNIX contributed significantly to their spread in academic and business environments, solidifying C's position as a fundamental language for system programming. By the late 1970s, C had already established itself as the preferred language for system software development, and its use was starting to expand into other areas of programming.

The 1980s: ANSI C Standardization

With the growing popularity of the C language, the need to standardize its syntax and functionality emerged. By the late 1970s, there were several variants of C, each with minor differences depending on the platform or compiler used. To resolve this fragmentation, the American National

Standards Institute (ANSI) created a committee in 1983 to develop a formal standard for the C language.

In 1989, this committee released the ANSI C standard, also known as C89. This standard precisely defined the syntax, standard library functions, and language behavior, ensuring that programs written in C could be compiled and run on different platforms without substantial modifications.

Later Developments

In the 1990s, the ANSI C standard was further developed, leading to the C99 version, which introduced new features such as support for higher-precision floating-point types, variable-length arrays, and the ability to declare variables anywhere within a code block. The next update, known as C11 (released in 2011), introduced further improvements such as support for concurrent programming and a more advanced error-handling system.

Today, the C language continues to be widely used, both in its original form and as the basis for other modern languages like C++ and C#. Its influence extends to languages like Java and Python, which have inherited many of its conceptual features.

Areas of Application of C

The C language is extremely versatile and is used in a wide range of applications due to its efficiency and ability to directly manage hardware resources. Here are some of the main areas where C is used:

1. **Operating Systems:** One of the most well-known uses of the C language is in the development of operating systems. UNIX, the first major operating system written in C, demonstrated that it was possible to create a portable OS using a high-level language. Since then, many operating systems, including Linux, Windows, and macOS, have been largely written using C (or languages based on

it, like C++).

2. **System Software Development:** C is also used for developing system software such as compilers, interpreters, and hardware drivers. Thanks to its ability to interact directly with hardware and manage resources like memory, C is ideal for writing code that requires precise control over system resources.

3. **Embedded Applications:** Many electronic devices, such as routers, microcontrollers, cars, and IoT (Internet of Things) devices, use C for their software. This is because C allows programmers to write programs that can run in resource-constrained environments (in terms of memory and processing power), providing a high level of efficiency and control.

4. **Low-level Programming and Drivers:** C is often used to write hardware drivers, programs that allow the operating system to communicate with external devices such as

printers, graphics cards, and other peripherals. Drivers require very precise control of the hardware, and C offers the necessary flexibility to implement such software.

5. **Cross-platform Application Development:** Thanks to the portability of C code, many applications that need to run on multiple platforms are written in this language. If an application is written in C following the appropriate standards, it can be compiled and executed on various hardware architectures and operating systems with few changes.

6. **Game Development:** While C++ is more commonly used in the game industry today, C still plays an important role, especially when it comes to low-level hardware aspects such as graphics and sound management. Many game engines are written in C or C++ due to their efficiency and execution speed.

Setting Up the Development Environment

To begin programming in C, you need to configure an appropriate development environment that allows you to write, compile, and run your programs. Setting up the development environment includes choosing an IDE (Integrated Development Environment), installing a C compiler, and configuring the environment correctly.

Choosing an IDE

An IDE is software that provides an integrated environment for writing and developing code. Modern IDEs offer a range of features that simplify the programming process, such as syntax highlighting, project management, debugging, and more.

Here are some of the main IDEs available for C development:

1. **Visual Studio Code:** Developed by Microsoft, Visual Studio Code is one of the most popular code editors in the world. It is lightweight, highly configurable, and supports a wide range of programming languages, including C.

2. **Code::Blocks:** Code::Blocks is a free and open-source IDE specifically designed for C and C++ languages.

3. **Eclipse IDE for C/C++ Developers:** A well-known IDE mainly for Java, but it also offers a version for C and C++ development.

4. **CLion:** A paid IDE developed by JetBrains, specifically designed for C and C++ development, with advanced features.

5. **Dev-C++:** Another free and open-source IDE for C and C++, especially good for beginners.

Installing Compilers

A compiler is essential for running C programs. The source code must be translated into machine language before execution. There are several C compilers available for different platforms:

1. **GCC (GNU Compiler Collection):** One of the most widely used compilers for the C language.

2. **Clang:** An alternative compiler to GCC, known for its speed and quality of error diagnostics.

3. **MSVC (Microsoft Visual C++):** The compiler provided by Microsoft for developing software in C and C++ on Windows.

4. **TinyCC:** A lightweight and fast compiler, useful for small projects or learning the C language.

Configuring the Environment

Once the IDE and compiler are chosen, the development environment needs to be properly configured to start writing C code.

2. Basic Concepts of the C Language

The C programming language forms the foundation of many modern languages and is widely used for system programming, embedded software, compilers, and much more. In this section, we will explore the fundamental concepts of C, covering syntax, data types, variables, operators, and input/output operations.

C Language Syntax

The syntax of the C language defines the rules that a programmer must follow to write correct code. These rules include how code blocks are defined, how variables are declared, how data types are used, and more. Below, we will explore some of the key components of C syntax.

1. **Basic C Program**

A C program has a basic structure that includes standard library inclusion, the declaration of the `main()` function, and the management of commands within curly braces `{}`. The following example represents a minimal C program that prints "Hello, World!":

```c
#include <stdio.h>  // Include the library for input/output

int main() {
    printf("Hello, World!\n");  // Print the string to the screen
    return 0;  // End the program and return 0
}
```

- **`#include <stdio.h>`**: This line includes the C standard input/output library. The `printf()` function used in the program is part of this library.

- **`int main()`**: The `main()` function is the entry point of the program. All the executed code must be contained within it.

- **`{}`**: Curly braces delimit a block of code. In the case of the `main()` function, they enclose the instructions to be executed.

- **`printf()`**: This function prints the text inside the parentheses.

- **`return 0;`**: Indicates that the program has successfully completed.

2. **Comments in Code**

C allows the inclusion of comments, which are parts of text ignored by the compiler, useful for making the code more readable. There are two types of comments in C:

- **Single-line comments**: Use `//` and continue to the end of the line.

```c
// This is a single-line comment
printf("Hello, World!\n");
```

- **Multi-line comments**: Delimited by `/*` and `*/`.

```c
/* This is a comment
   on multiple lines */
printf("Hello, World!\n");
```

3. **Identifiers**

Identifiers are names given to variables, functions, and other elements of the program.

They must follow these rules:

- Must start with a letter or an underscore (`_`).
- Can contain letters, numbers, and underscores.
- Are case-sensitive, so `variable` and `Variable` are different.

Example:

```c
int number;  // Valid identifier
int _counter;  // Valid identifier
int 2value;  // Invalid, cannot start with a number
```

Data Types and Variables

In the C language, **data types** define the kind of value a variable can hold. Every variable must be declared with a data type before it can be used. Let's review the main data types and how to declare variables.

1. **Primitive Data Types**

C provides several primitive data types:

- **int**: Integer type, used for whole numbers.

```c
int a = 5;
```

- **float**: Single-precision floating-point number (32-bit).

```c
float b = 3.14;
```

- **double**: Double-precision floating-point number (64-bit).

```c
double c = 3.1415926535;
```

- **char**: Character type, stores a single character (8-bit).

```c
char d = 'A';
```

- **void**: Type that indicates the absence of data. It is mainly used to specify that a function returns nothing.

2. **Derived Data Types**

In addition to primitive types, there are derived types like arrays, pointers, and structures. Here's an overview:

- **Array**: A sequence of elements of the same type.

```c
int array[5] = {1, 2, 3, 4, 5};
```

- **Pointers**: Variables that store the memory address of other variables.

```c
int x = 10;
int *p = &x;  // p is a pointer to x
```

- **Struct**: A composite data type that can contain variables of different types.

```c
struct Point {
    int x;
    int y;
};
```

3. **Declaring and Initializing Variables**

A variable must be declared before being

used. The declaration specifies the data type and the variable's name. It can also be initialized immediately with a value.

Example:

```c
int number;        // Declaration of an integer variable

number = 5;        // Assignment of a value

int another_number = 10;  // Declaration and initialization
```

4. **Type Modifiers**

In C, there are **modifiers** that affect the interpretation and memory used by primitive data types. The main modifiers are:

- **short**: Reduces the size of an integer type.

```c
short int short_value = 32767;
```

- **long**: Increases the size of an integer or float type.

```c
long int long_value = 2147483647;
```

- **signed**: Defines an integer type that can be positive or negative.

```c
signed int signed_number = -10;
```

```

- **unsigned**: Defines an integer type that can only be positive.

```c
unsigned int natural_number = 10;
```

Operators

Operators are symbols that instruct the compiler to perform mathematical, logical, or assignment operations. The main operators in C include:

1. **Arithmetic Operators**

Arithmetic operators allow mathematical operations on numeric variables. Here is a list
```

of basic arithmetic operators:

- **`+`**: Addition

 ```c
 int sum = 5 + 3; // Result: 8
 ```

- **`-`**: Subtraction

 ```c
 int difference = 5 - 3; // Result: 2
 ```

- **`*`**: Multiplication

 ```c
 int product = 5 * 3; // Result: 15
 ```

```

- **`/`**: Division

```c
int quotient = 6 / 3;  // Result: 2
```

- **`%`**: Modulo (remainder of integer division)

```c
int remainder = 5 % 2;  // Result: 1
```

Example:

```c

```
int a = 10, b = 3;

int result = a + b; // Addition
```

2. **Comparison Operators**

Comparison operators allow comparing two values and return a boolean value (true or false):

- **`==`**: Equality

    ```c
    if (a == b) { // Checks if a is equal to b
        // Code executed if true
    }
    ```

- **`!=`**: Inequality

```c
if (a != b) { // Checks if a is not equal to b
    // Code executed if true
}
```

- **`>`**: Greater than

```c
if (a > b) { // Checks if a is greater than b
    // Code executed if true
}
```

- **`<`**: Less than

```c
```

```
if (a < b) { // Checks if a is less than b
    // Code executed if true
}
```

- **`>=`**: Greater than or equal to

```c
if (a >= b) { // Checks if a is greater than or equal to b
    // Code executed if true
}
```

- **`<=`**: Less than or equal to

```c
if (a <= b) { // Checks if a is less than or equal to b
```

// Code executed if true
}
```

#### 3. **Logical Operators**

Logical operators are used to combine multiple conditions and return a boolean result:

- **`&&`**: Logical AND (true if both conditions are true)

```c
if (a > 0 && b > 0) { // True only if both conditions are true
   // Code executed if true
}
```
```

- **`||`**: Logical OR (true if at least one condition is true)

```c
if (a > 0 || b > 0) { // True if at least one condition is true
    // Code executed if true
}
```

- **`!`**: Logical NOT (inverts the boolean value)

```c
if (!(a > 0)) { // True if a is not greater than 0
    // Code executed if true
}
```

Basic Input/Output Operations

Input and output are fundamental to any program. In C, input is typically received from the keyboard, and output is displayed on the screen. The main functions to handle input and output are provided by the standard library `<stdio.h>`.

####

1. **Output: `printf()` Function**

The `printf()` function is used to print text and variables to the screen. The syntax is:

```c
printf("format string", variable1, variable2, ...);
```

```

Example:

```c
int number = 5;
printf("The value of number is %d\n", number);
```

In the format string, `%d` is a placeholder for an integer, and `\n` is a newline character.

Other placeholders:

- **`%f`**: For floating-point numbers.
- **`%c`**: For characters.
- **`%s`**: For strings.
```

2. **Input: `scanf()` Function**

The `scanf()` function reads input from the user and stores it in a variable. The syntax is:

```c
scanf("format string", &variable);
```

Example:

```c
int age;
scanf("%d", &age);  // Reads an integer from the user
```

The `&` symbol is used to pass the address of the variable where the input should be stored.

By understanding the above fundamental concepts, one can begin programming in C with confidence. These basic principles will serve as the foundation for more advanced topics like control structures, functions, and memory management.

3. Flow Control in C

Flow control is a key concept in any programming language, as it allows the program to make decisions and repeat actions based on certain conditions. In C, there are various statements that allow you to effectively control the flow of the program. In this section, we will explore **conditional statements**, **loops**, and **jump statements** in C, providing practical examples for each.

Conditional Statements

Conditional statements allow you to execute different blocks of code depending on whether a certain condition is true or false. In C, the main conditional statements are:

1. **`if`**

2. **`if-else`**

3. **`if-else if-else`**

4. **`switch-case`**

1. `if`

The `if` statement allows you to execute a block of code only if a specified condition is true. The syntax of the `if` statement is as follows:

```c
if (condition) {
    // Code executed if the condition is true
}
```

Example:

```c
#include <stdio.h>

int main() {
    int number = 10;

    if (number > 5) {
        printf("The number is greater than 5.\n");
    }

    return 0;
}
```

In this example, the program checks if `number` is greater than 5. If the condition is true, the message "The number is greater than 5." will be printed.

2. `if-else`

The `if-else` statement allows you to specify an alternative block of code to be executed if the condition is false. The syntax is as follows:

```c
if (condition) {
    // Code executed if the condition is true
} else {
    // Code executed if the condition is false
}
```

Example:

```c
```

```c
#include <stdio.h>

int main() {
    int number = 3;

    if (number > 5) {
        printf("The number is greater than 5.\n");
    } else {
        printf("The number is not greater than 5.\n");
    }

    return 0;
}
```

In this case, since `number` is less than 5, the code inside the `else` block will be executed, and the program will print "The number is not greater than 5."

3. `if-else if-else`

To handle multiple conditions in a sequence, you can use the `if-else if-else` statement. The syntax is as follows:

```c
if (condition1) {
    // Code executed if condition1 is true
} else if (condition2) {
    // Code executed if condition2 is true
} else {
    // Code executed if none of the previous conditions are true
}
```

Example:

```c
#include <stdio.h>

int main() {
    int number = 8;

    if (number > 10) {
        printf("The number is greater than 10.\n");
    } else if (number > 5) {
        printf("The number is greater than 5 but less than or equal to 10.\n");
    } else {
        printf("The number is less than or equal to 5.\n");
    }
```

```
    return 0;
}
```

In this example, since the value of `number` is 8, the condition `number > 5` is true, and the program will print "The number is greater than 5 but less than or equal to 10."

4. `switch-case`

The `switch` statement is useful when you have many conditions to check for the same value. Instead of writing multiple `if-else` statements, you can use a `switch` statement, which compares an expression against different options (`case`). The syntax is as follows:

```c
switch (expression) {
```

```
    case value1:
        // Code executed if expression == value1
        break;
    case value2:
        // Code executed if expression == value2
        break;
    default:
        // Code executed if no case matches
}
```

Example:

```c
#include <stdio.h>

int main() {
    int day = 3;
```

```c
    switch (day) {
        case 1:
            printf("Monday\n");
            break;
        case 2:
            printf("Tuesday\n");
            break;
        case 3:
            printf("Wednesday\n");
            break;
        default:
            printf("Invalid day\n");
    }

    return 0;
}
```

In this example, the variable `day` is compared to different values. Since `day` is equal to 3, the program prints "Wednesday."

Loops and Iteration

Loops allow you to repeatedly execute a block of code as long as a certain condition is true. In C, there are three main loop structures:

1. **`while`**
2. **`do-while`**
3. **`for`**

1. `while`

The `while` loop executes a block of code as long as the specified condition remains true. The syntax is as follows:

```c
while (condition) {
    // Code executed while the condition is true
}
```

Example:

```c
#include <stdio.h>

int main() {
    int i = 0;

    while (i < 5) {
```

```
        printf("i = %d\n", i);
        i++;
    }


    return 0;
}
```

In this example, the loop continues to execute the block of code as long as the value of `i` is less than 5. In each iteration, `i` is incremented by 1.

2. `do-while`

The `do-while` loop is similar to `while`, but with an important difference: the block of code is executed **at least once**, even if the condition is false. The syntax is as follows:

```c
do {
    // Code executed at least once
} while (condition);
```

Example:

```c
#include <stdio.h>

int main() {
    int i = 0;

    do {
        printf("i = %d\n", i);
        i++;
    } while (i < 5);
```

    return 0;

}
```


In this example, the loop prints the value of `i` and increments it by 1. The loop continues as long as `i` is less than 5. Even if the condition is initially false, the block of code would still be executed once.

#### 3. `for`

The `for` loop is particularly useful when you know in advance how many iterations you need to perform. The syntax is as follows:

```c
for (initialization; condition; increment) {
    // Code executed in each iteration

}
```

Example:

```c
#include <stdio.h>

int main() {
    for (int i = 0; i < 5; i++) {
        printf("i = %d\n", i);
    }

    return 0;
}
```

In this example, the `for` loop executes the
```

block of code as long as `i` is less than 5. In each iteration, `i` is incremented by 1.

Jump Statements

Jump statements allow you to alter the flow of program execution, skipping parts of the code or exiting loops. The main jump statements in C are:

1. **`break`**
2. **`continue`**
3. **`return`**

1. `break`

The `break` statement is used to exit a loop or a `switch-case` statement immediately. When executed, the program control jumps to the statement following the block that contains the `break`.

Example in a loop:

```c
#include <stdio.h>

int main() {
    for (int i = 0; i < 10; i++) {
        if (i == 5) {
            break;  // Exits the loop when i is equal to 5
        }
        printf("i = %d\n", i);
    }

    return 0;
```

    }
```

In this example, the `for` loop will be terminated when `i` reaches the value of 5.

Example in a `switch`:

```c
#include <stdio.h>

int main() {
    int day = 3;

    switch (day) {
        case 1:
            printf("Monday\n");
            break;

```c
        case 2:
            printf("Tuesday\n");
            break;
        case 3:
            printf("Wednesday\n");
            break;
        default:
            printf("Invalid day\n");
    }

    return 0;
}
```

In this example, the `break` ensures that only the matching `case` block for `day` is executed.

2. `continue`

The `continue` statement is used inside loops to skip the current iteration and move directly to the next one. When executed, the program control returns to the loop condition without executing the remaining code in the current iteration.

Example:

```c
#include <stdio.h>

int main() {
    for (int i = 0; i < 10; i++) {
        if (i == 5) {
            continue; // Skips the current iteration when i is equal to 5
        }
        printf("i = %d\n", i);
```

```
    }


    return 0;

}
```

In this example, when `i` is equal to 5, the `continue` statement is executed, and the program skips printing `i = 5`, continuing with the next iteration.

3. `return`

The `return` statement is used to immediately exit a function and return a value (if the function is not of type `void`). When executed, the program control returns to the function's caller.

Example:

```c
#include <stdio.h>

int sum(int a, int b) {
    return a + b;  // Returns the sum of a and b
}

int main() {
    int result = sum(3, 4);
    printf("The result is: %d\n", result);
    return 0;
}
```

In this example, the `sum` function returns the result of adding the two parameters `a` and `b`, which is then printed in the main program.

Flow control in C is fundamental for programming, as it allows you to write dynamic and responsive code. By using conditional statements, loops, and jump statements, you can manage the program's execution logic flexibly. We explored the main flow control structures, providing concrete examples to demonstrate their use. Understanding these concepts is essential for writing efficient and well-structured programs in C.

4. Functions in C

Functions are a fundamental component of the C language, allowing you to organize and structure code in a modular and reusable way. A function is a block of code that can be called from other parts of the program to perform a specific task. This makes the program easier to understand, maintain, and modify.

In this article, we will explore the following aspects of functions in C:

- Function declaration and definition

- Function parameters

- Recursive functions

- Inline functions

Function Declaration and Definition

In C, a function must be declared before it can be used. There are two main concepts related to functions:

1. **Declaration**: Informs the compiler of the function's name, return type, and parameters.

2. **Definition**: Provides the function's code, i.e., the body of the function that will be executed when the function is called.

Function Declaration

A function declaration, also called a **prototype**, tells the compiler that a function exists with a certain name, return type, and a list of parameters. The syntax is as follows:

```c

return_type function_name(parameter_type1 parameter_name1, parameter_type2
```

parameter_name2, ...);
```

Example of a function declaration:

```c
int sum(int a, int b);
```

This declaration indicates that there is a function named `sum` that takes two parameters of type `int` and returns a value of type `int`.

Function Definition

The **definition** of a function includes the function body, i.e., the code that will be executed when the function is called. The syntax is similar to the declaration, with the
```

addition of curly braces `{}` that enclose the function's code.

```c
return_type function_name(parameter_type1 parameter_name1, parameter_type2 parameter_name2, ...) {
    // Function body
}
```

Example of a function definition:

```c
int sum(int a, int b) {
    return a + b;
}
```

In this example, the `sum` function takes two integers `a` and `b` as input, calculates their sum, and returns the result.

Calling a Function

Once declared and defined, a function can be called in the main program or other functions. A function call involves passing the necessary values and receiving (if applicable) the return value.

Example of a function call:

```c
#include <stdio.h>

int sum(int a, int b) {
    return a + b;
}
```

```c
int main() {
    int result = sum(5, 3);
    printf("The sum is: %d\n", result);
    return 0;
}
```

In this example, the `sum` function is called in `main()` with parameters `5` and `3`. The return value is stored in the variable `result` and printed to the screen.

Function Parameters

Functions can accept **parameters** or **arguments** that are passed when the function is called. Parameters make functions more flexible and reusable.

Pass-by-Value Parameters

In C, parameters are usually passed **by value**, meaning that a copy of the value is passed to the function. Changes to the parameters inside the function do not affect the original values in the calling program.

Example:

```c
#include <stdio.h>

void increment(int x) {
    x = x + 1;
    printf("Value of x inside the function: %d\n", x);
}
```

```c
int main() {
    int a = 10;
    increment(a);
    printf("Value of a in main: %d\n", a);
    return 0;
}
```

Output:

```
Value of x inside the function: 11
Value of a in main: 10
```

In this example, the value of `a` is not modified in `main()`, because `a` is passed by value and the function `increment` operates on a copy of `a`.

Pass-by-Reference Parameters (Using Pointers)

If you want a function to modify the original values of the parameters, you need to pass **pointers** to the parameters. This way, the function works directly with the address of the original variable.

Example:

```c
#include <stdio.h>

void increment(int *x) {
    *x = *x + 1;
}
```

```c
int main() {
    int a = 10;
    increment(&a);
    printf("Value of a in main after the function: %d\n", a);
    return 0;
}
```

Output:

```
Value of a in main after the function: 11
```

In this example, the `increment` function modifies the original value of `a` by passing a pointer to `a`.

Functions with Multiple Parameters

Functions can accept multiple parameters, separated by commas. When calling the function, the values of the arguments must be passed in the corresponding order.

Example:

```c
#include <stdio.h>

int multiply(int a, int b) {
    return a * b;
}

int main() {
    int result = multiply(4, 5);
    printf("The result of multiplication is:
```

```
%d\n", result);
    return 0;
}
```

Output:

```
The result of multiplication is: 20
```

In this example, the `multiply` function takes two integer parameters and returns their product.

Recursive Functions

A **recursive function** is a function that calls itself. Recursion is useful for solving problems that can be broken down into smaller subproblems of the same type.

For recursion to work correctly, you need to define:

1. A **base case**, which terminates the recursion.

2. A **recursive step**, which reduces the problem to a simpler problem.

Recursive Function Example: Factorial

The **factorial** of a positive integer `n`, denoted as `n!`, is the product of all positive integers less than or equal to `n`. For example, `5! = 5 * 4 * 3 * 2 * 1 = 120`.

A recursive function to calculate the factorial can be written as follows:

```c
#include <stdio.h>

int factorial(int n) {
    if (n == 0 || n == 1) {
        return 1;  // Base case
    } else {
        return n * factorial(n - 1);  // Recursive step
    }
}

int main() {
    int number = 5;
    printf("The factorial of %d is: %d\n", number, factorial(number));
    return 0;
}
```

```

Output:

```

The factorial of 5 is: 120

```

In this example, the `factorial` function calls itself, progressively reducing the value of `n` until it reaches the base case (`n == 0` or `n == 1`).

#### Recursive Function Example: Fibonacci

The Fibonacci sequence is a numerical sequence where each number is the sum of the two previous numbers, with the first two numbers being 0 and 1. The recursive function to calculate the `n`th Fibonacci number can be written as follows:
```

```c
#include <stdio.h>

int fibonacci(int n) {
    if (n == 0) {
        return 0; // Base case
    } else if (n == 1) {
        return 1; // Base case
    } else {
        return fibonacci(n - 1) + fibonacci(n - 2); // Recursive step
    }
}

int main() {
    int number = 6;
    printf("The %dth Fibonacci number is: %d\n", number, fibonacci(number));
```

        return 0;

}
```


Output:

```

The 6th Fibonacci number is: 8

```

In this example, the `fibonacci` function calls itself to calculate the two previous numbers in the sequence and sum them.

#### Advantages and Disadvantages of Recursion

**Advantages**:

- Recursion is often a natural way to solve
```

problems that can be broken down into similar subproblems.

- Recursive code tends to be more concise and readable, especially for complex problems like tree or graph traversal.

Disadvantages:

- Recursion can consume more memory than an iterative solution because each recursive call requires a new stack frame.

- If not handled correctly, it can lead to **infinite recursion**, resulting in a stack overflow error.

Inline Functions

Inline functions are a feature introduced in the C99 standard, which allows you to suggest to the compiler to "inline" the function code directly at the point where the function is called, instead of making an actual function call. This can improve performance by eliminating the overhead of a function call, but it is up to the compiler to decide whether to respect the suggestion.

Inline Function Declaration

The `inline` keyword is used to indicate to the compiler that you want the function to be expanded inline. The syntax is as follows:

```c
inline return_type function_name(parameter_type1 parameter_name1, ...) {
   // Function body
}
```

Example of an inline function:

```c
#include <stdio.h>

inline int square(int x) {
    return x * x;
}

int main() {
    int number = 5;
    printf("The square of %d is: %d\n", number, square(number));
    return 0;
}
```

In this example, the `square` function could be expanded inline by the compiler, meaning the code `x * x` could be inserted directly at the point where the function is called.

Advantages and Disadvantages of Inline Functions

Advantages:

- Improves performance by eliminating the overhead of function calls, especially for simple, small functions.

- Reduces the need for jumps in the code, potentially improving data locality in the cache.

Disadvantages:

- Excessive use of inline functions can increase the size of the binary code (a problem known as **code bloat**).

- Not all functions are suitable for inlining,

especially those that are very complex or contain loops and heavy operations.

Functions in C are a powerful tool for structuring and organizing code in a modular, reusable, and maintainable way. We have explored various aspects of functions, including their declaration, definition, the use of parameters, and recursive functions. Finally, we introduced inline functions, which offer potential performance improvements in certain cases.

Understanding functions and their features is essential for writing efficient and well-structured programs in C and is a key skill for any developer working with this language.

5.Arrays, Strings, and Pointers

In C, **arrays** and **strings** are fundamental components for data management. An array is a collection of elements of the same type, while strings are arrays of characters terminated by the null character (`\0`). Arrays allow the organized handling of data sets, and strings simplify text management.

Declaration and Initialization of Arrays

An array in C is a sequence of elements of the same type. Declaring an array requires specifying the data type and the number of elements it will contain.

Declaring an Array

The syntax for declaring an array is as follows:

```c
type array_name[size];
```

For example:

```c
int numbers[5];  // Array of 5 integers
char letters[10];  // Array of 10 characters
```

Initializing an Array

Arrays can be initialized during their declaration. If fewer values than specified are provided, the remaining elements are set to zero (for numeric types).

Example:

```c
int numbers[5] = {1, 2, 3, 4, 5};  // Full initialization
int other_numbers[5] = {1, 2};  // Only the first two elements are initialized, others are 0
```

It's also possible to leave the square brackets empty, allowing the compiler to determine the size based on the number of provided values:

```c
int values[] = {10, 20, 30};  // Size is automatically 3
```

Accessing Array Elements

Array elements are indexed starting from zero. Accessing the elements is done using the index.

Example:

```c
#include <stdio.h>

int main() {
    int numbers[3] = {10, 20, 30};
    printf("The first element is: %d\n", numbers[0]);
    printf("The second element is: %d\n", numbers[1]);
    printf("The third element is: %d\n", numbers[2]);
    return 0;
}
```

Multidimensional Arrays

Arrays can have multiple dimensions. A **two-dimensional array** can be thought of as a matrix with rows and columns. A three-dimensional array can be seen as an array of arrays.

Declaring a Two-Dimensional Array

```c
int matrix[3][4]; // Matrix with 3 rows and 4 columns
```

Initializing a Two-Dimensional Array

Multidimensional arrays can be initialized similarly to one-dimensional arrays.

Example:

```c
int matrix[2][3] = {
    {1, 2, 3},
    {4, 5, 6}
};
```

Accessing Multidimensional Array Elements

Elements of a multidimensional array are indexed using two or more indices. For example:

```c
#include <stdio.h>
```

```c
int main() {
    int matrix[2][3] = {
        {1, 2, 3},
        {4, 5, 6}
    };
    printf("Element at row 1, column 2: %d\n", matrix[0][1]);
    return 0;
}
```

This program will print `2`, as the index `[0][1]` refers to the first row and the second column.

Manipulating Strings

In C, **strings** are treated as arrays of characters terminated by the null character (`\0`). The null character signals the end of the string, allowing for variable-length strings within fixed-size arrays.

Declaring and Initializing Strings

A string can be declared as an array of characters:

```c
char name[6] = {'H', 'e', 'l', 'l', 'o', '\0'};
```

Alternatively, you can use a more compact form:

```c
char name[] = "Hello";  // The compiler
```

automatically adds '\0'
```

#### String Manipulation Functions

C provides several functions for working with strings, found in the `<string.h>` library. Some of these include:

- **`strlen()`**: Returns the length of a string (excluding the `\0` character).
- **`strcpy()`**: Copies a string to another.
- **`strcat()`**: Concatenates two strings.
- **`strcmp()`**: Compares two strings.

Example using some of these functions:

```c
#include <stdio.h>

```c
#include <string.h>

int main() {
    char name[20] = "Hello";
    char addition[] = " World";

    printf("Length of '%s': %lu\n", name, strlen(name));

    strcat(name, addition);  // Concatenates " World" to "Hello"
    printf("After concatenation: %s\n", name);

    return 0;
}
```
```

Output:
```

```
Length of 'Hello': 5
After concatenation: Hello World
```

Pointers

Pointers are an advanced feature in C that allows working directly with memory addresses. Understanding pointers is essential for writing efficient and flexible code, especially when working with arrays, functions, and complex structures.

Concept of a Pointer

A pointer is a variable that contains the address of another variable. The data type of a pointer is determined by the type of the variable it points to.

Example of pointer declaration:

```c
int *p; // Pointer to an integer
```

The **`&`** operator returns the address of a variable, while the **`*`** (dereference) operator returns the value stored at the pointed address.

Example:

```c
#include <stdio.h>
```

```c
int main() {
    int var = 10;
    int *pointer = &var;  // Assigns the address of 'var' to the pointer

    printf("Value of var: %d\n", var);
    printf("Address of var: %p\n", (void*)pointer);
    printf("Value pointed by the pointer: %d\n", *pointer);

    return 0;
}
```

Output:

```
Value of var: 10
```

Address of var: 0x7ffeedab7b04

Value pointed by the pointer: 10
```

#### Pointer Operations

Common pointer operations include:

- **Dereferencing**: accessing the value pointed to by a pointer using `*`.

- **Pointer arithmetic**: incrementing or decrementing a pointer to access the next elements of an array.

Example:

```c
#include <stdio.h>

int main() {

```c
    int numbers[] = {10, 20, 30};
    int *p = numbers;  // The pointer points to the first element of the array

    printf("First element: %d\n", *p);  // Dereferencing
    p++;  // Pointer arithmetic (incrementing the address of an integer)
    printf("Second element: %d\n", *p);

    return 0;
}
```

Output:

```
First element: 10
Second element: 20
```

```

#### Pointers and Arrays

Arrays in C are closely related to pointers. The address of the first element of an array is equivalent to the address of the array itself. For example, given an array `numbers`, the pointer `numbers` points to the first element.

Example:

```c
#include <stdio.h>

int main() {
    int numbers[] = {5, 10, 15};
    int *p = numbers;  // Pointer to the first element of the array

```c
    for (int i = 0; i < 3; i++) {
        printf("Element %d: %d\n", i, *(p + i));
    }

    return 0;
}
```

In this example, the pointer is used to access the array elements through pointer arithmetic.

Pointers and Functions

Pointers can be passed to functions, allowing the functions to modify the original variable values directly.

Example:

```c
#include <stdio.h>

void increment(int *p) {
    (*p)++;
}

int main() {
    int x = 10;
    increment(&x);  // Pass the address of x
    printf("Value of x after increment(): %d\n", x);  // Output: 11
    return 0;
}
```

In this case, the `increment` function directly modifies the value of `x` using a pointer.

Arrays, strings, pointers, and structures are fundamental components of the C language. Understanding these concepts is essential for writing efficient and well-structured code. Unions and user-defined types complete the set of tools available to C developers for creating complex and well-organized programs.

6. Memory Management in C

Memory management in C is a crucial aspect that involves reserving, allocating, deallocating, and manipulating memory. The C language provides both static memory management (at compile time) and dynamic memory management (at runtime). Dynamic memory is particularly useful for applications that require creating data structures of variable sizes, and proper memory management is essential to avoid issues like memory leaks or illegal access.

Dynamic Memory Allocation

Dynamic memory allocation in C allows you to request memory during program execution and release it when it's no longer needed. This is handled through functions from the `<stdlib.h>` library.

Allocation Functions

The main functions for dynamic memory allocation are:

- **`malloc()`**: Allocates a block of memory of specified size and returns a pointer to the first byte of the block. The allocated memory is uninitialized.

- **`calloc()`**: Allocates memory for a specified number of elements and initializes all bytes to zero.

- **`realloc()`**: Resizes a previously allocated block of memory.

- **`free()`**: Deallocates a previously allocated block of memory.

Dynamic Allocation Examples

`malloc()`

```c
```

```c
#include <stdio.h>
#include <stdlib.h>

int main() {
    int *array;
    int n = 5;

    array = (int *)malloc(n * sizeof(int)); // Allocates memory for an array of 5 integers

    if (array == NULL) { // Checks if the allocation succeeded
        printf("Insufficient memory\n");
        return 1;
    }

    for (int i = 0; i < n; i++) {
        array[i] = i + 1;
    }
```

```c
    for (int i = 0; i < n; i++) {
        printf("Element %d: %d\n", i, array[i]);
    }

    free(array);  // Frees the allocated memory
    return 0;
}
```

`calloc()`

```c
#include <stdio.h>
#include <stdlib.h>

int main() {
    int *array;
```

```c
    int n = 5;

    array = (int *)calloc(n, sizeof(int));  // Allocates memory for 5 integers and initializes to zero

    if (array == NULL) {
        printf("Insufficient memory\n");
        return 1;
    }

    for (int i = 0; i < n; i++) {
        printf("Element %d: %d\n", i, array[i]);
    }

    free(array);
    return 0;
}
```

`realloc()`

```c
#include <stdio.h>
#include <stdlib.h>

int main() {
    int *array;
    int n = 5;

    array = (int *)malloc(n * sizeof(int));

    if (array == NULL) {
        printf("Insufficient memory\n");
        return 1;
    }
```

```c
for (int i = 0; i < n; i++) {
    array[i] = i + 1;
}


// Resizes the array to 10 elements
n = 10;
array = (int *)realloc(array, n * sizeof(int));

if (array == NULL) {
    printf("Insufficient memory\n");
    return 1;
}


for (int i = 5; i < n; i++) {
    array[i] = i + 1;
}


for (int i = 0; i < n; i++) {
```

```
        printf("Element %d: %d\n", i, array[i]);
    }


    free(array);
    return 0;
}
```

Avoiding Memory Leaks

A **memory leak** occurs when dynamically allocated memory is never deallocated. This can happen if the reference to the allocated memory block is lost, preventing it from being freed. To avoid memory leaks, it's important to:

- **Free memory** when it's no longer needed using `free()`.
- **Check pointer validity** before using

them.

- Use memory debugging tools such as **Valgrind** to identify and resolve memory leaks.

Example of a memory leak:

```c
#include <stdlib.h>

int main() {
    int *ptr = (int *)malloc(100 * sizeof(int));  // Memory allocation

    // The reference to ptr is lost without freeing the memory

    ptr = NULL;  // Memory leak: allocated memory is never freed

    return 0;
}
```

In this example, the memory allocated with `malloc()` is never freed, resulting in a memory leak.

File Handling and Input/Output

File handling and input/output (I/O) operations in C are performed through a series of functions provided by the standard library `<stdio.h>`. These functions allow opening, closing, reading, and writing files.

Basic File Operations

In C, files are handled using the `FILE*` type, and file operations are carried out through standard functions.

Opening and Closing Files

Opening a File

To open a file, use the `fopen()` function, which returns a pointer to a `FILE` if the opening is successful or `NULL` if there is an error.

```c
FILE *file = fopen("example.txt", "r"); // Opens the file in read mode
if (file == NULL) {
    printf("Error opening the file.\n");
    return 1;
}
```

Common file opening modes are:

- `"r"`: Opens for reading.

- `"w"`: Opens for writing (creates a new file or truncates an existing file).

- `"a"`: Opens for appending (adds data to the end of the file).

- `"r+"`: Opens for reading and writing.

- `"w+"`: Opens for reading and writing (creates a new file or truncates an existing file).

- `"a+"`: Opens for reading and writing (adds data to the end of the file).

Closing a File

To close an opened file, use the `fclose()` function:

```c
fclose(file); // Closes the file
```

Reading and Writing Files

Reading a File

To read data from a file, you can use the functions `fgetc()`, `fgets()`, or `fread()`.

```c
#include <stdio.h>

int main() {
    FILE *file = fopen("example.txt", "r");
    if (file == NULL) {
        printf("Error opening the file.\n");
        return 1;
    }
```

```
    char c;
    while ((c = fgetc(file)) != EOF) {
        putchar(c);  // Prints the character read
    }

    fclose(file);
    return 0;
}
```

Writing to a File

To write data to a file, you can use the functions `fputc()`, `fputs()`, or `fwrite()`.

```c
#include <stdio.h>
```

```c
int main() {
    FILE *file = fopen("example.txt", "w");
    if (file == NULL) {
        printf("Error opening the file.\n");
        return 1;
    }

    fprintf(file, "Hello, world!\n");  // Writes a string to the file

    fclose(file);
    return 0;
}
```

Complete Example of Reading and Writing

```c
```

```c
#include <stdio.h>

int main() {
    // Writing to a file
    FILE *file = fopen("example.txt", "w");
    if (file == NULL) {
        printf("Error opening the file for writing.\n");
        return 1;
    }

    fprintf(file, "This is a line of text.\n");
    fclose(file);

    // Reading from the file
    file = fopen("example.txt", "r");
    if (file == NULL) {
        printf("Error opening the file for reading.\n");
```

```c
        return 1;
    }

    char buffer[100];
    while (fgets(buffer, sizeof(buffer), file) != NULL) {
        printf("%s", buffer);  // Prints the line read
    }

    fclose(file);
    return 0;
}
```

Memory management and file handling are fundamental skills in C. Dynamic memory allocation provides flexibility in managing data, but it requires careful attention to avoid problems like memory leaks. File manipulation allows reading and writing data to disk, which is essential for most software applications. Using these features correctly allows you to write robust and efficient programs.

7. Preprocessor and Directives in C

The **preprocessor** is a crucial phase in the compilation of C code. It operates before the actual compilation phase and handles directives, macros, and other operations that influence the source code before it is turned into machine code. Preprocessor directives are used to make modifications to the code, include files, and define macros.

Preprocessor Directives

Preprocessor directives are special commands that begin with the `#` symbol and are not followed by a semicolon. They are used to instruct the preprocessor on how to handle the source code.

File Inclusion

The `#include` directive is used to include

header files. Header files can contain function declarations, macro definitions, and common data structures.

- **`#include <file>`**: Includes a file from the system directory.
- **`#include "file"`**: Includes a file from the current directory.

Usage example:

```c
#include <stdio.h> // Includes the standard library for input and output

int main() {
    printf("Hello, world!\n");
    return 0;
}
```

In this example, the header file `stdio.h` is included to enable the use of the `printf()` function.

Macro Definition

Macros are text replacements that are substituted into the source code by the preprocessor. They are defined using `#define` and can be simple text substitutions or more complex ones with parameters.

- **Simple macro definition**:

```c
#define PI 3.14159
```

In this example, `PI` will be replaced with

`3.14159` whenever it appears in the code.

- **Macros with parameters**:

```c
#define SQUARE(x) ((x) * (x))
```

Usage:

```c
#include <stdio.h>

int main() {
    int value = 5;
    printf("The square of %d is %d\n", value, SQUARE(value));
    return 0;
```

}
```

In this example, `SQUARE(value)` will be replaced with `((value) * (value))` during preprocessing.

##### Conditional Compilation

Conditional directives allow including or excluding parts of code based on certain conditions. Some of the most common directives are:

- **`#if` and `#endif`**: Check if a condition is true and include the code only if the condition is met.

- **`#ifdef` and `#ifndef`**: Check if a macro is defined or not defined.

- **`#else` and `#elif`**: Provide alternatives to `#if` conditions.
```

Example of using conditional directives:

```c
#define DEBUG

#ifdef DEBUG
   #include <stdio.h>
#endif

int main() {
   #ifdef DEBUG
      printf("Debug mode active\n");
   #endif
   return 0;
}
```

In this example, the `printf` statement is compiled only if `DEBUG` is defined.

Macros and Header Files

Macros and **header files** are closely related in C programming. Header files (`.h`) contain declarations and definitions that can be used across multiple source files (`.c`).

Macros in Header Files

Macros are often used in header files to provide constants and inline functions. Here's an example of a header file with macros:

math_util.h

```c
#ifndef MATH_UTIL_H
```

```
#define MATH_UTIL_H

#define PI 3.14159
#define SQUARE(x) ((x) * (x))

#endif // MATH_UTIL_H
```

main.c

```c
#include <stdio.h>
#include "math_util.h"

int main() {
    printf("The value of PI is %f\n", PI);
    printf("The square of 4 is %d\n", SQUARE(4));
```

    return 0;

}
```

In this example, `math_util.h` is included in `main.c`, and the defined macros are used in the program.

##### Conditional Inclusion

Conditional inclusion prevents multiple inclusions of a header file. This is done using guard macros like `#ifndef`, `#define`, and `#endif`.

**file.h**

```c
#ifndef FILE_H
#define FILE_H

// Declarations and definitions

#endif // FILE_H
```

In this example, the contents of `file.h` will be included only once, even if the file is included multiple times in different source files.

Advanced Programming

Advanced programming in C involves using techniques and tools to handle complex data, manage errors, and organize code modularly.

Complex Data Types
```

C allows the creation and management of **complex data types** using structures, unions, and enumerations.

Structures

Structures (`struct`) allow grouping of variables of different types under a single name.

Example of a complex structure:

```c
#include <stdio.h>

typedef struct {
    char name[50];
    int age;
```

```
    float height;
} Person;

int main() {
    Person p1 = {"Anna", 30, 1.75};
    printf("Name: %s\n", p1.name);
    printf("Age: %d\n", p1.age);
    printf("Height: %.2f\n", p1.height);
    return 0;
}
```

Unions

Unions (`union`) allow storing different types of data in the same memory space.

Example of a union:

```c
#include <stdio.h>

union Data {
    int integer;
    float decimal;
    char string[20];
};

int main() {
    union Data d;
    d.integer = 10;
    printf("Integer: %d\n", d.integer);

    d.decimal = 3.14;
    printf("Decimal: %f\n", d.decimal);
```

```c
    snprintf(d.string, sizeof(d.string), "Test");
    printf("String: %s\n", d.string);

    return 0;
}
```

Enumerations

Enumerations (`enum`) define a set of symbolic values for a variable.

Example of an enumeration:

```c
#include <stdio.h>

enum DaysOfWeek {
```

    MONDAY, TUESDAY, WEDNESDAY, THURSDAY, FRIDAY, SATURDAY, SUNDAY
};

int main() {

    enum DaysOfWeek today = WEDNESDAY;

    printf("Today is day number %d of the week.\n", today);

    return 0;
}
```

#### Error Handling

**Error handling** in C can be done by checking return values of functions and using global error variables like `errno`.
```

Checking Return Values

Many standard library functions return special values to indicate errors. It is important to check these values to handle errors appropriately.

Example of error checking:

```c
#include <stdio.h>
#include <stdlib.h>

int main() {
    FILE *file = fopen("non_existent_file.txt", "r");
    if (file == NULL) {
        perror("Error opening file");
        return 1;
```

```
    }
    fclose(file);
    return 0;
}
```

In this example, `perror()` prints a descriptive error message based on the value of `errno`.

Using `errno`

The global variable `errno` is used to signal errors in library functions. It contains specific values for different types of errors.

Example:

```c
#include <stdio.h>
```

```c
#include <errno.h>
#include <string.h>

int main() {
    FILE *file = fopen("another_non_existent_file.txt", "r");
    if (file == NULL) {
        printf("Error: %s\n", strerror(errno));
        return 1;
    }
    fclose(file);
    return 0;
}
```

In this example, `strerror(errno)` returns a descriptive string of the error.

Modular Programming

Modular programming helps to break down a complex program into smaller, manageable modules. This is achieved through the use of source files and header files.

Module Separation

A modular program is divided into source files (`.c`) and header files (`.h`). Each source file contains function implementations, while header files contain declarations.

math_utils.h

```c
#ifndef MATH_UTILS_H
#define MATH_UTILS_H
```

```c
int add(int a, int b);
int subtract(int a, int b);

#endif // MATH_UTILS_H
```

math_utils.c

```c
#include "math_utils.h"

int add(int a, int b) {
    return a + b;
}

int subtract(int a, int b) {
    return a - b;
}
```

```

**main.c**

```c
#include <stdio.h>
#include "math_utils.h"

int main() {
    int a = 5, b = 3;
    printf("Sum: %d\n", add(a, b));
    printf("Difference: %d\n", subtract(a, b));
    return 0;
}
```

In this example, `math_utils.c` and `math_utils.h` define and declare the functions `add` and `subtract`, and `main.c` uses them.
```

C Standard and Compatibility

The C language has undergone various evolutions over time, and there have been different standards that have influenced the language's compatibility and features.

Differences between ANSI C and K&R C

K&R C (Kernighan and Ritchie) is the original version of the C language described in the book "The C Programming Language" by Kernighan and Ritchie. **ANSI C** (American National Standards Institute C) is the first official standard for the language, published in 1989 and also known as C89 or C90.

Key Differences:

- **Function Prototypes**: ANSI C introduces function prototype declarations, which were not present in K&R C.

- **Data Types**: ANSI C standardizes data types like `int`, `char`, `float`, and `double`, and introduces the `void` type.

- **Library Functions**: ANSI C specifies a standard set of libraries and functions, such as `<stdlib.h>`, `<stdio.h>`, and `<string.h>`, which were not standardized in K&R C.

Example of a function prototype in ANSI C:

```c
int add(int a, int b);  // Function prototype
```

K&R C does not require function prototypes, and function declarations are made only during their definition.

Variants of the C Language

In addition to C89/C90, there have been other standards:

- **C99**: Introduces new features such as `long long` data types, variables declared within blocks, and inline functions.

- **C11**: Adds improvements such as thread management, atomic types, and security enhancements.

- **C18**: Provides minor corrections and improvements over C11 without introducing new features.

Example of C99 feature:

```c
#include <stdio.h>

int main() {
    int x = 10;
    {
        int y = 20;  // Variable declared inside a block
        printf("y: %d\n", y);
    }
    // printf("y: %d\n", y);  // Error: y is not visible here
    return 0;
}
```

Compilation and Portability

Compilation and **portability** are important aspects of the C language. A C program must be compiled into machine code to be executed on a computer. Portability refers to the ability to run the same source code on different platforms without modifications.

Compilation

A C compiler translates source code into object code and then into an executable file. Example of a compilation command with `gcc`:

```bash
gcc -o program main.c
```

This command compiles the source file `main.c` and produces an executable called `program`.

Portability

To ensure that C code is portable, it is important to follow language standard specifications and avoid dependencies on specific compiler or operating system implementations. Using standard libraries and testing code on different platforms helps ensure portability.

Example of portable code:

```c
#include <stdio.h>

int main() {
    printf("Hello, world!\n");
    return 0;
}
```

```

This simple code uses only standard libraries and can be compiled and run on any system that supports the C language.

---

The preprocessor and directives in C provide powerful tools for source code manipulation, file inclusion, and macro definition. Advanced C programming involves managing complex data and implementing techniques for error handling and modular programming. Understanding the differences between C standards, language variants, and portability issues is essential for developing robust and compatible code across different platforms. With these tools and knowledge, you can write efficient, modular, and portable C programs.
```

8.Practical Examples in C

The C language is widely used for a variety of applications, ranging from simple to complex ones. Its ability to manipulate memory at a low level and its efficiency make it ideal for projects requiring high performance. We will explore examples of simple and complex projects, common data structures, and real-world applications to provide an overview of how C can be used in different situations.

Simple and Complex Projects

Simple Projects

1. Basic Calculator

A simple and common project is a basic calculator that can perform arithmetic operations such as addition, subtraction, multiplication, and division.

Code:

```c
#include <stdio.h>

int main() {
    char operation;
    double num1, num2, result;

    printf("Enter operation (+, -, *, /): ");
    scanf(" %c", &operation);

    printf("Enter two numbers: ");
    scanf("%lf %lf", &num1, &num2);

    switch (operation) {
        case '+':
```

```c
        result = num1 + num2;
        break;
    case '-':
        result = num1 - num2;
        break;
    case '*':
        result = num1 * num2;
        break;
    case '/':
        if (num2 != 0) {
            result = num1 / num2;
        } else {
            printf("Error: division by zero.\n");
            return 1;
        }
        break;
    default:
        printf("Invalid operation.\n");
```

```
        return 1;
    }


    printf("Result: %.2lf\n", result);
    return 0;
}
```

In this example, we use a `switch` statement to handle different arithmetic operations based on user input.

2. Array Sorting

Another simple project is sorting an array of numbers using the bubble sort algorithm.

Code:

```c
#include <stdio.h>

void bubbleSort(int arr[], int n) {
    int i, j, temp;
    for (i = 0; i < n - 1; i++) {
        for (j = 0; j < n - i - 1; j++) {
            if (arr[j] > arr[j + 1]) {
                // Swap arr[j] and arr[j + 1]
                temp = arr[j];
                arr[j] = arr[j + 1];
                arr[j + 1] = temp;
            }
        }
    }
}

int main() {
```

```
    int arr[] = {64, 34, 25, 12, 22, 11, 90};
    int n = sizeof(arr) / sizeof(arr[0]);

    bubbleSort(arr, n);

    printf("Sorted array: \n");
    for (int i = 0; i < n; i++) {
        printf("%d ", arr[i]);
    }
    printf("\n");

    return 0;
}
```
```

In this example, the bubble sort algorithm is used to sort an array of integers in ascending order.
```

Complex Projects

1. Simple Database Management

A more complex project could involve managing a simple in-memory database. This example implements a data structure to store and manage user records.

Code:

```c
#include <stdio.h>
#include <stdlib.h>
#include <string.h>

#define MAX_NAME 50
#define MAX_USERS 100
```

```c
typedef struct {
    char name[MAX_NAME];
    int age;
} User;

User database[MAX_USERS];
int count = 0;

void addUser(const char *name, int age) {
    if (count < MAX_USERS) {
        strncpy(database[count].name, name, MAX_NAME - 1);
        database[count].name[MAX_NAME - 1] = '\0'; // Ensure string termination
        database[count].age = age;
        count++;
    } else {
        printf("Database is full!\n");
    }
```

```c
}


void printDatabase() {
    for (int i = 0; i < count; i++) {
        printf("Name: %s, Age: %d\n", database[i].name, database[i].age);
    }
}


int main() {
    addUser("Alice", 30);
    addUser("Bob", 25);

    printf("User database:\n");
    printDatabase();

    return 0;
}
```

```

In this example, a simple database is created to store and manage user records using a structure and an array. The `addUser` and `printDatabase` functions handle adding and displaying data.

**2. Advanced Data Structure Implementation: Binary Search Tree**

A complex project might include advanced data structures like a binary search tree (BST). This example implements insertion and search operations in a binary search tree.

**Code:**

```c
#include <stdio.h>
#include <stdlib.h>
```
```

```c
typedef struct Node {
    int value;
    struct Node *left;
    struct Node *right;
} Node;

Node* createNode(int value) {
    Node *newNode = (Node*)malloc(sizeof(Node));
    newNode->value = value;
    newNode->left = NULL;
    newNode->right = NULL;
    return newNode;
}

Node* insert(Node *root, int value) {
    if (root == NULL) {
```

```c
        return createNode(value);
    }

    if (value < root->value) {
        root->left = insert(root->left, value);
    } else {
        root->right = insert(root->right, value);
    }

    return root;
}


int search(Node *root, int value) {
    if (root == NULL) {
        return 0;
    }
    if (root->value == value) {
        return 1;
```

```c
    }
    if (value < root->value) {
        return search(root->left, value);
    } else {
        return search(root->right, value);
    }
}


void freeTree(Node *root) {
    if (root != NULL) {
        freeTree(root->left);
        freeTree(root->right);
        free(root);
    }
}


int main() {
    Node *root = NULL;
```

```c
    root = insert(root, 50);
    insert(root, 30);
    insert(root, 70);
    insert(root, 20);
    insert(root, 40);
    insert(root, 60);
    insert(root, 80);

    printf("Search 40: %s\n", search(root, 40) ? "Found" : "Not found");
    printf("Search 90: %s\n", search(root, 90) ? "Found" : "Not found");

    freeTree(root);
    return 0;
}
```

In this example, we implement a binary search

tree with functions to insert and search values, and a function to free the memory used by the tree.

Debugging and Optimization

Debugging and **optimization** are crucial aspects of software development. Debugging helps identify and resolve errors in the code, while optimization aims to improve the performance of the program.

Debugging Techniques

1. Using `printf` for Debugging

One of the simplest debugging techniques is inserting `printf` statements to trace the flow of the program and the values of variables.

Example:

```c
#include <stdio.h>

int compute(int a, int b) {
    printf("a = %d, b = %d\n", a, b);
    return a + b;
}

int main() {
    int result = compute(5, 3);
    printf("Result = %d\n", result);
    return 0;
}
```

In this example, `printf` statements are used to print variable values and the result of the function.

2. Using a Debugger

Debugging tools like **GDB** (GNU Debugger) offer advanced features for stepping through the program, examining variables, and setting breakpoints.

Example of Using GDB:

```bash
gcc -g -o program main.c
gdb ./program
```

In the GDB prompt, you can use commands like `break`, `run`, `next`, `print`, and `continue` to debug the program.

GDB Commands:

```gdb
(gdb) break main
(gdb) run
(gdb) next
(gdb) print variable
(gdb) continue
```

3. Analyzing Core Dumps

When a program crashes, it may generate a core dump file. Analyzing the core dump can provide information about the program's state at the time of the crash.

Command to Enable Core Dumps:

```bash
ulimit -c unlimited
```

Example of Analysis with GDB:

```bash
gdb ./program core
```

Code Optimization

1. Optimizing Computational Complexity

Optimizing algorithms to reduce their computational complexity can significantly improve the performance of the program.

Example of Optimization:

Use binary search instead of linear search for sorted arrays.

Linear Search:

```c
int linearSearch(int arr[], int n, int value) {
    for (int i = 0; i < n; i++) {
        if (arr[i] == value) {
            return i;
        }
    }
    return -1;
}
```

```

**Binary Search:**

```c
int binarySearch(int arr[], int n, int value) {
    int start = 0;
    int end = n - 1;

    while (start <= end) {
        int mid = start + (end - start) / 2;

        if (arr[mid] == value) {
            return mid;
        }
        if (arr[mid] < value) {
            start = mid + 1;
        } else {

```
        end = mid - 1;
      }
    }
    return -1;
}
```

2. Memory Optimization

Reducing memory usage and improving efficiency can lead to faster and less resource-intensive programs.

Example of Memory Optimization:

Use appropriate data types and efficient data structures.

Using `unsigned int` to Limit Negative Values:

```c
unsigned int add(unsigned int a, unsigned int b) {
    return a + b;
}
```

3. Compiler Optimization

Modern compilers offer optimization options that can enhance the performance of the generated code.

Example of Optimization Options with GCC:

```bash
gcc -O2 -o program main.c
```

The `-O2` option enables a set of optimizations that improve performance without compromising the correctness of the program.

Profiling Tools

Profiling helps identify code areas that consume the most resources and focus optimization efforts.

1. Using `gprof`

gprof is a profiling tool that can analyze the performance of a program.

Example of Profiling with gprof:

```bash
gcc -pg -o program main.c
./program
gprof ./program gmon.out > report.txt
```

2. Using `valgrind`

Valgrind is a useful tool for detecting memory leaks and memory access issues.

Example of Analysis with Valgrind:

```bash
valgrind --leak-check=full ./program
```

3. Using `perf`

perf is a Linux profiling tool that provides detailed performance information.

Example of Profiling with perf:

```bash
perf record ./program
perf report
```

4. Profiling with IDE Tools

Many integrated development environments (IDEs) offer built-in profiling tools that can simplify performance analysis.

Example with Visual Studio:

In Visual Studio, you can use the performance profiler to collect and view data on your program's performance.

Practical examples in C range from simple projects like calculators and array sorting to complex projects like database managers and advanced data structures. Knowledge of debugging and optimization techniques is essential for developing robust and high-performance software. Tools such as `gdb`, `valgrind`, `perf`, and `gprof` facilitate debugging and profiling, while code and memory optimization helps improve the efficiency and performance of programs. With these skills, C programmers can tackle a wide range of challenges and develop high-quality applications.

9. Comprehensive Glossary of C

The C language is rich in technical terminology that can be complex for newcomers. This glossary provides an overview of the main definitions and concepts used in C.

A

- **Algorithm**: A sequence of logical and defined steps to solve a problem or perform a task.

- **Array**: A collection of variables of the same type, accessible via an index. Arrays can be one-dimensional or multi-dimensional.

- **Assignment**: The operation of assigning a value to a variable using the assignment operator `=`.

B

- **Break**: A flow control statement that terminates a `for`, `while`, or `do-while` loop prematurely.

- **Binary Tree**: A data structure consisting of nodes, where each node has at most two children, one to the left and one to the right.

C

- **Cast**: The explicit conversion of a data type to another using the syntax `(type) variable`.

- **Char**: A data type in C that represents a single character. `char` typically occupies 1 byte of memory.

- **Const**: A type modifier that indicates that the value of a variable cannot be modified after its initialization.

- **Control Flow**: Control structures such as `if`, `else`, `switch`, `for`, `while`, and `do-while` that determine the execution flow of the program.

- **Compiler**: A program that translates source code written in C into executable machine code.

D

- **Debugging**: The process of identifying and fixing errors in the source code.

- **Dynamic Memory Allocation**: Techniques for allocating and freeing memory during the program's execution using functions like `malloc`, `calloc`, `realloc`, and `free`.

- **Directive**: A preprocessor instruction that begins with `#`, such as `#include` and `#define`.

E

- **Enumeration (Enum)**: A data type consisting of a set of named integer constants. Defined with the `enum` keyword.

- **Expression**: A combination of variables, constants, operators, and functions that produces a value.

F

- **File**: A memory unit that can contain data, source code, or other types of information. In C, files are managed through the standard input/output library (`<stdio.h>`).

- **Function**: A block of code that performs a specific task and can return a value. Functions can accept parameters and are declared and defined using the syntax `return_type function_name(parameters)`.

G

- **Global Variable**: A variable declared outside of all functions and accessible from any function in the program.

- **Goto**: A statement that transfers control to a specified label in the code. The use of `goto` is generally discouraged due to the difficulty of maintaining code.

H

- **Header File (.h)**: A file that contains function declarations, macros, and type definitions that can be included in other source files via the `#include` directive.

I

- **If Statement**: A conditional statement that executes a block of code if a condition is true.

- **Initialization**: The process of assigning an initial value to a variable at the time of declaration.

- **Inline Function**: A function that is expanded directly at the call site by the compiler to avoid the overhead of function calls. Declared with the `inline` keyword.

J

- **Jump Statement**: A statement that alters the flow of control in the program, such as `break`, `continue`, and `goto`.

L

- **Loop**: A flow control structure that repeats a block of code as long as a condition is true. The main types of loops in C are `for`, `while`, and `do-while`.

- **Library**: A collection of predefined functions and routines that can be used in C programs. Standard libraries are included via `#include` directives.

M

- **Macro**: A text definition replaced by the preprocessor before compilation, defined with

`#define`. Macros can be simple constants or inline functions.

- **Main Function**: The entry point of every C program. The `main` function is the first function executed, and the program terminates when `main` finishes.

N

- **Null Pointer**: A pointer that does not point to any valid memory location. In C, it is represented by `NULL`.

O

- **Operator**: A symbol representing a mathematical or logical operation to be performed on data. Operators in C include `+`, `-`, `*`, `/`, `==`, and `&&`.

- **Overloading**: The concept of having multiple functions with the same name but different parameters. However, C does not support function overloading.

P

- **Pointer**: A variable that stores the memory address of another variable. Pointers are used for direct memory manipulation.

- **Preprocessor**: The compiler phase that performs replacements of directives like `#include`, `#define`, and `#if` before actual compilation.

- **Prototype**: A function declaration specifying the return type and parameter types without providing the implementation. Example: `int sum(int a, int b);`

R

- **Recursion**: The technique where a function calls itself directly or indirectly. Each function call must approach a termination condition to avoid infinite loops.

- **Return Statement**: A statement that ends the execution of a function and returns a value to the caller.

S

- **Static Variable**: A variable that retains its value between function calls where it is declared, and its visibility is limited to the block in which it is declared.

- **Struct (Structure)**: A user-defined data type that can contain variables of different types under a single name. Defined with the `struct` keyword.

- **String**: A sequence of characters terminated by a null character (`\0`). In C, strings are represented as arrays of characters.

T

- **Type**: The definition of a set of values and the operations that can be performed on them. Examples include `int`, `float`, `char`, and `struct`.

- **Typecasting**: The explicit conversion of a variable from one data type to another. Example: `(int) variable`.

U

- **Union**: A user-defined data type in which all members share the same memory space. Only one member can hold a valid value at any given time. Defined with the `union` keyword.

- **Undefined Behavior**: A situation where the behavior of the program is not specified by the C standard, which can lead to unpredictable results or errors.

V

- **Variable**: A memory area with a name that can hold data and whose value can be modified during program execution.

- **Void**: A special type indicating the absence of a value. Used to declare functions that do not return a value and to define pointers to generic types.

W

- **While Loop**: A type of loop that continues to execute a block of code as long as a condition is true. The syntax is `while (condition) { /* code */ }`.

X

- **XOR Operator**: A bitwise operator that returns 1 if one, but not both, of the corresponding bits are 1. In C, it is represented by `^`.

Y

- **Yield**: In C, there is no specific construct called `yield` as in other languages, but it generally refers to the behavior of a function that returns a value or result.

Z

- **Zero-based Indexing**: The practice of numbering array indices starting from 0. For example, the first element of an array has an index of 0.

This glossary provides an overview of key definitions and concepts in the C language, aiding in understanding and learning C.

Index

1. Introduction pg.4

2. Basic Concepts of the C Language pg.17

3. Flow Control in C pg.40

4. Functions in C pg.64

5. Arrays, Strings, and Pointers pg.86

6. Memory Management in C pg.105

7. Preprocessor and Directives in C pg.123

8. Practical Examples in C pg.151

9. Comprehensive Glossary of C pg.178

www.ingramcontent.com/pod-product-compliance
Lightning Source LLC
Chambersburg PA
CBHW052155220526
45471CB00004B/1681